ASTRONOMY

Every Galaxy Has a BLACK HOLE

Dr Bryson Gore

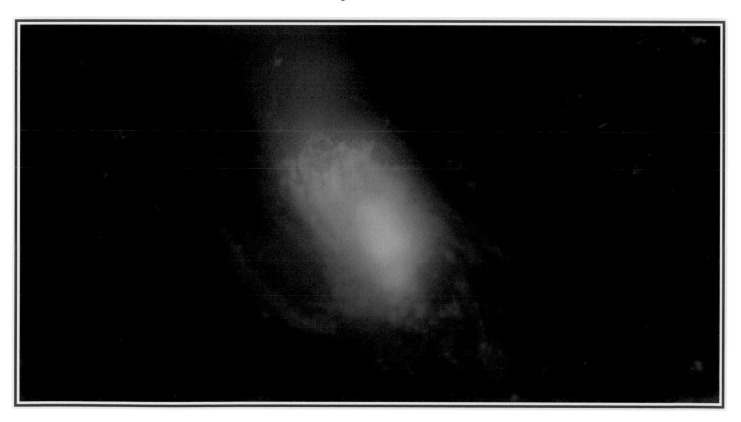

Aladdin/Watts
London • Sydney

CONTENTS

© Aladdin Books Ltd 2005

Designed and produced by
Aladdin Books Ltd
2/3 Fitzroy Mews
London W1T 6DF

First published in
Great Britain in 2005 by
Franklin Watts
96 Leonard Street
London EC2A 4XD

ISBN 0 7496 5522 4

Editor: Katie Harker
Design: Flick, Book Design
and Graphics
Illustrators: Q2A Creative

The author, Dr Bryson Gore, is
a freelance lecturer and science
demonstrator, working with the
Royal Institution and other
science centres in the UK.

A catalogue record for this
book is available from the
British Library.

Printed in Malaysia

Picture research: Brian Hunter Smart

Photocredits:
Abbreviations: l-left, r-right, b-
bottom, t-top, c-centre, m-middle
Front cover l, back cover r, 8-9,
16br, 18 both, 26mr — Corbis. 1,
8mrt, 11bl, 16-17, 25tl, 31bl —
NASA. 4mr, 7br, 13br, 23bl —
Courtesy NASA/JPL - Caltech. 8mrb,
8br — NASA and The Hubble
Heritage Team. 14mr — NASA
Johnson Space Center - Earth
Sciences and Image Analysis
(NASA-JSC-ES&IA). 20-21, 31br —
Flick Smith. 27mr — NASA/NSSDC.

Introduction

Humans have practised ASTRONOMY – the science of space –
for hundreds of thousands of years. Over time, our star gazing has
discovered many things about the nature of our Solar System and
the hidden depths of the Universe – but many secrets of space
are still waiting to be discovered.

In ancient times, the work of astronomers was based upon simple
observation with the naked eye. The Greeks observed points of light
that appeared to move among the stars. They called these objects
'planets' (meaning 'wanderers'), and we later named the planets after
Roman deities like 'Jupiter' and 'Mars'. The Greeks also observed comets
with sparkling tails and stars apparently falling from the
sky. Years later, scientists began to apply
mathematics to their observations to create
general theories about the Universe.

After 1600 AD, the invention of the telescope enabled people to observe details of space never seen before. But by the 20th century, humans were not content with general theories and observations – they wanted to witness the wonders of space first-hand. Initially no one believed in rocket science, but advances in machinery during the Second World War meant that rockets broke the grip of the Earth's gravity and later travelled to the Moon and to other planets. Since the 1950s and 1960s, satellites, space probes, space stations and human-crewed expeditions have brought spectacular developments in our understanding of the Universe.

This book takes a look at twelve of the most amazing astronomical developments that have taken place through history. Find out more about famous astronomers like William Herschel and Giovanni Cassini and learn how they used their skills to make sense of the night sky. By consulting fact boxes such as 'The science of...' and 'How do we know?' you will begin to understand more about the ways in which we have pieced together the story of the stars and the galaxies. Learn about our Sun and its Solar System, the planets and their moons, and the stars and galaxies that together form the whole of our Universe.

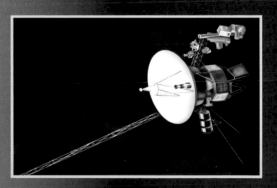

THE UNIVERSE BEGAN WITH A BIG BANG

Today, it is believed that the Universe and all the material in it exploded out of a minute volume of space about 10,000 to 15,000 million years ago. Scientists believe that this explosion – which they call the 'Big Bang' – happened in a fraction of a second. The effects of the blast were so strong that the Universe has been expanding ever since, with all the atoms, stars and galaxies moving apart from each other.

The Big Bang theory has been supported by the discovery of a background glow throughout space. Today, the glow is a colour that we can't see with the naked eye. However, scientists believe that thousands of millions of years ago the sky would have been lit up by a glow from the Big Bang.

HOW DO WE KNOW?

About 100 years ago, scientists began to measure how fast galaxies were travelling towards or away from the Earth, using a phenomenon called the 'Doppler Shift' (see page 7). They were surprised to find that almost every galaxy was travelling away from us. What's more, they found that the further a galaxy was from the Earth, the faster it was travelling. Galaxies situated a billion light-years from Earth were receding at about 20 million metres per second!

When scientists calculated the position of galaxies in history, they found that EVERYTHING would have been in the same place about 13,000 million years ago. This led astronomers to propose that the Universe began with a huge explosion – or 'Big Bang'.

Have you noticed how the sound of a police siren changes as the car approaches and then passes you? Scientists call this effect the 'Doppler Shift' – a phenomenon discovered by Christian Doppler (1803-1853).

One useful consequence of the Doppler Shift (which holds for light as well as sound waves) is that it reveals that galaxies and stars are moving away from the Solar System. This shows that the Universe is expanding. When light coming from a distant galaxy is seen through a spectroscope (an instrument that separates light rays into different colours), the light is shifted towards the red end of the colour spectrum. This redder light has a lowered frequency and is equivalent to the lowered pitch of a receding police car. The change in colour also indicates a difference in speed.

Although scientists are pretty certain that the Big Bang took place, they are far less certain about what happened before it. Did everything come out of nothing? Or did all the material rush inwards, collide and rebound, producing what scientists call a 'Big Bounce'? These questions still baffle cosmologists today.

Gravity is a force which causes all objects in space to attract each other – and this force increases with the size and proximity of an object. Until recently, scientists assumed that galaxies were slowing down due to a pull of gravity from the Universe. But it actually looks like they are speeding up! Will the Universe expand forever? Or will the force of gravity eventually become too powerful and pull all the contents of the Universe into a small region of space – what scientists call a 'Big Crunch'?

OUR UNIVERSE CONTAINS OVER 100 BILLION GALAXIES

When you look into the depths of the sky on a clear night you can see thousands of stars twinkling above you. Although you may not realise it, you can also see six or seven galaxies. These galaxies look very like stars, but in fact they are collections of gas, dust and billions of stars (see page 10). Scientists have estimated that the entire Universe contains over 100 billion galaxies.

1

HOW DO WE KNOW?

Most galaxies are not visible to the naked eye because they are so far away and very faint. Some galaxies are also obscured from our vision by large dust clouds in space. However, by using modern telescopes and special cameras, astronomers have been able to detect the presence of millions of galaxies in the sky.

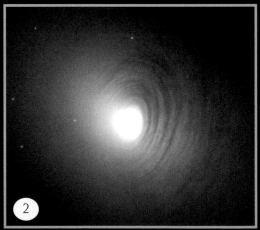

2

Nobody has ever counted the total number of stars and galaxies in the Universe – there are just too many! However, astronomers have counted how many stars and galaxies there are in a lot of small areas. They have then estimated the total number of stars and galaxies in the Universe by assuming that the rest of the sky has a similar concentration. In fact, scientists know that this is not entirely true – some regions have more galaxies than others.

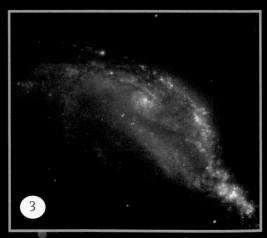

3

Stars and galaxies formed after the Big Bang when the force of gravity (see page 7) pulled clouds of gas and dust together.

The Earth and our Sun are located within a common spiral galaxy. Because we are inside our own galaxy we don't see it like any of the pictures on this page – when we look outwards through our galaxy we simply see a scattering of stars across the sky. We call this band the 'Milky Way'.

Astronomers have found that the Milky Way is part of a cluster of six or seven galaxies, most of which are only visible in the southern hemisphere. This cluster has a mixture of spiral, elliptical and irregular galaxies which are situated within about three million light-years of each other. The next nearest galaxy cluster is about 50 million light-years away. The gravitational attraction between galaxies in a cluster can distort them and sometimes they even collide. This gives rise to the shapes of galaxies that we see in space.

There are three basic types of galaxies. Our galaxy – the Milky Way – is a **spiral galaxy (1)**. It was formed when spinning balls of gas collapsed due to the pull of gravity. Spiral galaxies are often relatively flat like a pancake or a pizza.

Elliptical galaxies (2) are formed when spiral galaxies collide. There is very little rotation in an elliptical galaxy so it doesn't collapse down to a pancake.
Irregular galaxies (3) are formed when one galaxy nearly collides with another.

EVERY GALAXY HAS A BLACK HOLE AT ITS CENTRE

The Universe is full of galaxies – collections of gas, dust and billions of stars that have been drawn together by the effect of gravity. It is now widely believed that the pull of gravity causes galaxies to collapse at the centre, forming a 'black hole' – just like water being sucked down a plug-hole. Black holes are the true monsters of space. If enough material comes together in one place, the pull of gravity is so great that nothing can escape. Not even light.

THE SCIENCE OF...

When a galaxy forms, the centre (where most of the matter collects) becomes very dense and forms a massive star. This star can sometimes be millions of times bigger than our Sun and, at its centre, a black hole can form.

Stars are huge balls of hydrogen gas and dust that are held together by gravity. As this gas and dust is drawn inwards the star's temperature increases, causing hydrogen to be converted to helium (see page 12). For most of a star's life, this energy release balances the inward pull of gravity. However, as the star runs out of hydrogen, the pull of gravity eventually overpowers the release of energy. The star begins to contract and, as the outer layers fall inward, the core is compressed and heats to billions of degrees Celsius (°C).

If the star originally contains more than about five times the mass of our Sun, it explodes in a supernova (see page 18) and the outer layers are blown away into space. What remains is a highly compressed, and extremely large core. The core's gravity is so strong that it continues to collapse and literally disappears from view. Scientists call this disappearing core a 'black hole'.

WOWZSAT!

ALTHOUGH OUR OWN SUN IS A BIG STAR (WITH A DIAMETER OF 1.4 MILLION KM) IT IS NOT BIG ENOUGH TO TURN INTO A BLACK HOLE. THE SUN WOULD ONLY FORM A BLACK HOLE IF IT WERE SQUEEZED INTO A SPACE JUST 6 KM ACROSS.

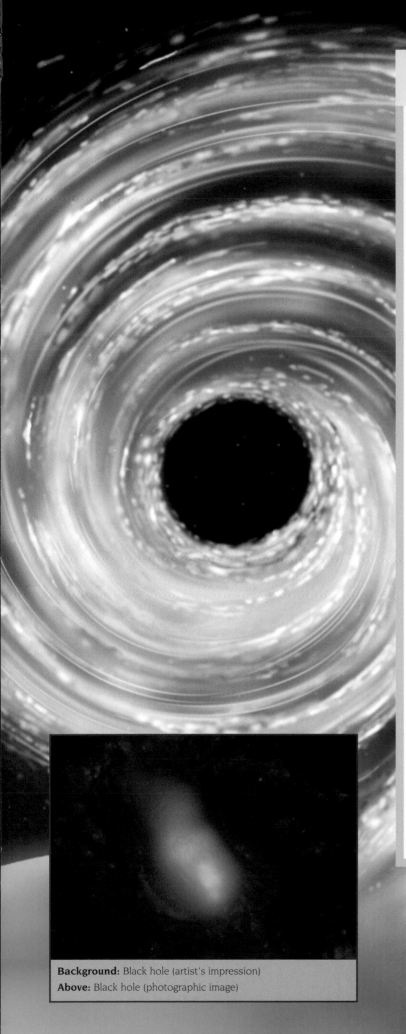

How do we know?

Light rays cannot escape the immense pull of gravity in a black hole so we'll never be able to see them! However, astronomers are pretty certain that black holes exist because they have seen the effect that they have on other objects in space. In the 1990s, scientists were surprised when telescopic observations

revealed that stars near a galaxy's centre were moving far faster than expected. Their findings suggested that a vast amount of matter must be concentrated at the heart of a galaxy, providing a gravitational force strong enough to keep the stars in orbit.

Other strange happenings in outer space have been attributed to black holes. A star might 'wobble' or spin, without visible explanation. Astronomers believe this could be due to the gravity of a nearby black hole. X-rays, jets of gas and bright lights seen coming from the centre of galaxies are also thought to be caused by superheated gas and material being pulled into a black hole.

Background: Black hole (artist's impression)
Above: Black hole (photographic image)

THE CENTRE OF THE SUN IS OVER 15 MILLION °C

That is very, very hot! So hot in fact, that it's difficult to imagine what it must be like. The Sun is a star just like all the stars that you see in the night sky. But the Sun is the hottest natural object in the Solar System. Without the Sun's high temperature our planet wouldn't have the right heat and light conditions to sustain life.

1. 6,000 °C = SURFACE OF THE SUN
2. 24,000 °C = LIGHTNING BOLT
3. 15,000,000 °C = NUCLEAR EXPLOSION

2.

THE SCIENCE OF...

The Sun is a star – a big mass of hydrogen gas that is pulled together by gravity. When most objects are squeezed together, their temperature increases. The weight of all the parts of the Sun pressing on the centre leads to very high temperatures and these temperatures cause the hydrogen atoms to collide at incredibly high speeds.

When the centre of the Sun rises to over 10 million °C it becomes like a giant nuclear reactor. Atoms at the centre travel at about 500 km per second – so fast that when they collide they stick together to form heavier atoms of helium. This process (called 'fusion') releases the energy that illuminates and heats our Solar System. It takes four hydrogen atoms to make one helium atom. This takes place in a number of steps – two hydrogen atoms collide to form deuterium (a heavy kind of hydrogen). Two deuterium atoms then collide to form helium.

As the Sun's core turns hydrogen into helium, it loses about one per cent of its matter as energy. This energy heats the Sun's core to over 15 million °C. It takes more than a million years for heat at the Sun's core to travel to the surface. At the surface, the Sun radiates heat and light energy away into space. We know from the Sun's colour that the temperature of the Sun's surface is 'only' about 6,000 °C (see page 14).

WOWZSAT!

THE SUN HAS ALREADY USED UP ABOUT HALF OF ITS HYDROGEN. IN ANOTHER 5 BILLION YEARS THE SUN WILL BEGIN TO DIE – IT WILL COOL, SHRINK AND EVENTUALLY FADE AWAY. BUT THIS IS STILL BILLIONS OF YEARS AWAY!

How do we know?

We can't measure the temperature of the Sun directly because no space probe would ever survive the extreme temperatures there!

However, by looking at the effects of gravity on a big cloud of hydrogen gas, researchers have estimated that for a ball of gas the size of our Sun, the pressure at the core is 250,000 million times greater than the pressure of our atmosphere. This pressure would result in a temperature of 15 million °C.

On average, each cubic metre of the Sun releases about the same amount of heat as a candle. However, the Sun contains about 1,000 million, million, million, million cubic metres of gas! Every second the Sun loses a million times more energy than humans use in one year.

3.

The Sun's temperature provides our Earth with the ideal conditions for life. With the exception of Mars, other planets in the Solar System are too cold or too hot for living things to grow. Mars (below) is the closest planet to Earth – scientists are still investigating whether there is evidence of life there.

Betelgeuse is one of the stars in the constellation of Orion (below). Betelgeuse is a 'Red Giant'. It is about 500 times bigger than our own Sun and has a surface temperature of 3,000 °C .

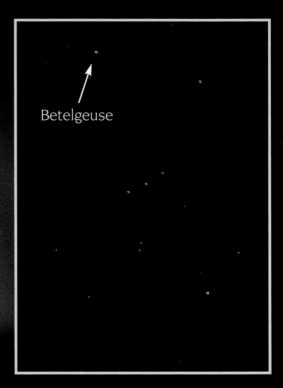

Betelgeuse

Y OU CAN TELL HOW HOT A STAR IS BY LOOKING AT ITS COLOUR

When astronomers first began to study the night sky they were interested in the brightness of the stars and where they were located. Then, about 100 years ago, they discovered that they could also measure the temperature of the stars and how fast the stars were moving (see page 6). All these findings have helped us to understand more about the properties of stars.

HOW DO WE KNOW?

Over 100 years ago, scientists realised that light is a type of heat, or energy. An object at 6,000 °C, like our Sun, gives out most of its heat as yellow light, with smaller amounts of red and blue.

Light is a type of wave that can travel across space. The wavelength of yellow light is about 600 nanometres (nm) (see page 30). Blue light is about 400 nm and red light about 800 nm.

The main colour given off by an object has a wavelength that is proportional to temperature. Most of the light emitted from Betelgeuse has a wavelength of 1,200 nm – a cooler colour that we can't see with our eyes. We call this colour infra-red, which means 'redder than red'!

The colour of our Sun tells us that it has a surface temperature of about 6,000 °C. The filament of a light bulb is about 3,000 °C and a candle flame is about 1,200 °C.

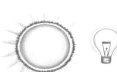

THE SCIENCE OF...

Any material will glow and give out light if you heat it up, whatever its 'normal' colour. If an object is at room temperature we cannot see this glow with our eyes, but once something is at about 600 °C it begins to glow a dull red. The hotter it becomes the brighter it gets and the light also becomes bluer (blue/white hot is hotter than red hot).

Most stars are like our Sun. Smaller stars tend to be colder, dimmer and redder. Heavier stars tend to be hotter, brighter and bluer in colour. Blue stars are hotter because the gravity pulling the gas together makes them burn faster. For this reason we find that big stars tend to come to the end of their lives faster than small ones.

These 'Blue Giants' are much bigger than our Sun, over 20 times the mass and have a surface temperature of more than 20,000 °C. Betelgeuse is an unusual star because it is big and red (not big and blue). Betelgeuse is at the end of its life and instead of exploding as a supernova (see page 18) it has expanded to form a 'Red Giant' which is slowly cooling over millions of years.

J UPITER IS LIKE A STAR THAT FAILED TO IGNITE

About 5,000 million years ago, an area of gas on the outer edge of a spiral galaxy began to collapse as the force of gravity pulled it together. Because the gas was spinning, centrifugal force prevented it from falling into a single point and, instead, it formed a disc. The material in this disc clumped together to form what we know today as the planets of our Solar System (of which Jupiter is one) and our Sun.

THE SCIENCE OF...

Over time the smaller planets of our Solar System – those that had a smaller force of gravity – lost all the lighter atoms back into space and were left with a rocky surface. The bigger planets held on to their atoms. We call these planets the 'gas giants' – Jupiter, Saturn, Uranus and Neptune. Meanwhile, the gas at the centre of the disc continued to fall in on itself. The moving atoms created friction which caused the gas to heat to 10 million °C and nuclear fusion created a star – our Sun (see page 12).

Jupiter is made from a very similar mix of atoms to our Sun. Although Jupiter's gravitational force is large enough to hold on to hydrogen atoms, it cannot squeeze them tightly enough to fuse them – the surface pressure on Jupiter is 'only' 100 million times the atmospheric pressure on Earth! Jupiter has a small rocky core that is covered by solid hydrogen. This core is then covered with liquid hydrogen and then a large ball of almost pure hydrogen gas. If Jupiter had 100 times more mass (just four times the diameter) it would have turned into a star like our Sun.

Like the other gas giants, Uranus has an atmosphere composed of mostly hydrogen, followed by helium and a little methane.

16

How do we know?

We understand the way that our Solar System formed from computer modelling. When we model a gas cloud in a computer, we begin with hundreds of millions of atoms moving freely in space. Then we get the computer to work out what would happen over millions of years as the particles are attracted by gravity and bump into each other.

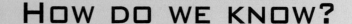

Computer models show that different sorts of solar systems form depending on how the atoms begin their journey. All solar systems have at least one star at the centre where most of the atoms collect. Sometimes the system forms two stars that orbit each other; these are called binary stars. About half the stars that you see in the sky are binary stars – the stars are just too close together to be seen as separate points of light.

When a single star is formed, it is surrounded by between 4 and 12 planets of varying sizes. The largest planets form gas giants, the smaller ones lose all their gases and form rocky planets like Mercury, Venus, Earth, Mars and Pluto.

WOWZSAT!

JUPITER IS THE LARGEST PLANET – SO BIG THAT ALL THE OTHER PLANETS IN OUR SOLAR SYSTEM COULD FIT INSIDE IT. IF IT WERE ANY BIGGER IT MIGHT BECOME TOO HOT IN THE MIDDLE, START TO GLOW AND TURN INTO ANOTHER SUN.

WE ARE ALL MADE OF STARDUST

Your body is made from dozens of different kinds of atoms such as hydrogen, oxygen, carbon and iron. The Earth is also made from a similar selection of atoms and has a core that is pure liquid iron. But where did all these atoms come from? Scientists have discovered that the Earth, and all the things on it, are made from the dust of stars that died thousands of millions of years ago.

The Big Bang created lots of light gases (like hydrogen and helium), but for billions of years stars have been making heavier atoms (like carbon and iron) by squeezing these light atoms together (see page 12). We now understand that an ordinary star like our Sun cannot make atoms that are heavier than iron. But many heavy atoms can be found on Earth and other planets – so where did they come from?

THE SCIENCE OF...

Scientists believe that heavier atoms like gold and silver were made in a series of gigantic explosions (called supernovae) at the end of the life of some very large stars. A supernova causes a single burst of energy, which makes a star thousands of millions of times brighter than it was during its lifetime. For a few days a supernova can shine more brightly than all the billions of other stars in its galaxy combined. Supernovae release debris which we call 'nebulae'.

Astronomers think that stars like these exploded more than 5,000 million years ago. The heavy atoms that were released mixed with hydrogen gas in space and cooled to form the ball of gas that collapsed to form our Sun and the planets, like Earth, that orbit it (see page 16).

A supernova was observed in July 1054 AD and today we call the debris from that explosion the 'Crab Nebula'. The Crab Nebula is still moving so fast that we can see differences in the shape of the nebula today from photographs that were taken 100 years ago.

A supernova (top).
The gaseous pillars of the
Eagle Nebula (bottom).

18

How do we know?

All the matter in the Universe was present in the Big Bang, but it only formed into atoms a few minutes afterwards – before that the Universe was too hot. Computer models have shown that roughly three minutes after the Big Bang itself, the temperature of the Universe had cooled rapidly enough to produce four new, light kinds of atoms – helium, lithium, beryllium and boron. If we look at the Universe today, hydrogen makes up about 73 per cent, helium about 24 per cent, and all the other elements about 2 per cent – the content of the Universe has changed very little since the Big Bang!

We now know that all the atoms that are lighter than iron originate from the stars. Stars in the early Universe were bigger and hotter, so they burned faster. But they only converted 10 to 20 per cent of their hydrogen into atoms like carbon, nitrogen, oxygen and iron. All atoms heavier than iron originated from exploding stars. When dust from a supernova mixes with interstellar gas, the heavier atoms collide and – over millions of years – they begin to form larger and larger clumps of rock. Scientists estimate that it took around 200 million years for the Earth to form in this way.

WOWZSAT!

SUPERNOVAE WERE VERY COMMON WHEN THE UNIVERSE WAS MORE DENSE. WHEN OUR SUN FORMED, THE UNIVERSE WAS NEARLY FOUR TIMES AS DENSE AS IT IS NOW. TWICE AS LONG AGO, IT WAS NEARLY TEN TIMES DENSER!

The Earth weighs about six thousand, billion, billion tonnes

Have you ever travelled in an aeroplane and looked down from the window? If so, you will probably have wondered at the immense expanse of planet Earth. The Earth must certainly be very large to accommodate the current world population of more than six billion people! Over the years, researchers have discovered that the Earth has a circumference of 40,000 km and a surface area of 0.5 billion square km. We've also discovered that the Earth is a very heavy planet.

6,000,000,000,000,000,000,000 tonnes

THE SCIENCE OF...

The Earth has a mass of six thousand, billion, billion tonnes, but in fact it weighs nothing at all! How can this be? Although weight and mass mean almost the same thing on Earth, scientists recognise that these two measurements are very different things. Mass tells us how hard it is to make something move and is measured in kilogrammes (1 tonne = 1,000 kg). Weight is the force with which an object is pulled downwards, and is measured in newtons (N).

Gravity makes things with mass pull towards each other. Normally, a large object (the Earth) pulls smaller objects (you) to produce weight. But in space the force of gravity is much weaker. An object may have a mass of 1 kg, but in space it would not push down on a set of weighing scales – it would be weightless!

With what force does the Earth pull on the Earth? Nothing! How then do we measure the mass of the Earth? The answer is that we measure what is known as 'G' – the gravitational constant. Combining the gravitational constant with a knowledge of the Earth's diameter enables scientists to calculate the Earth's mass.

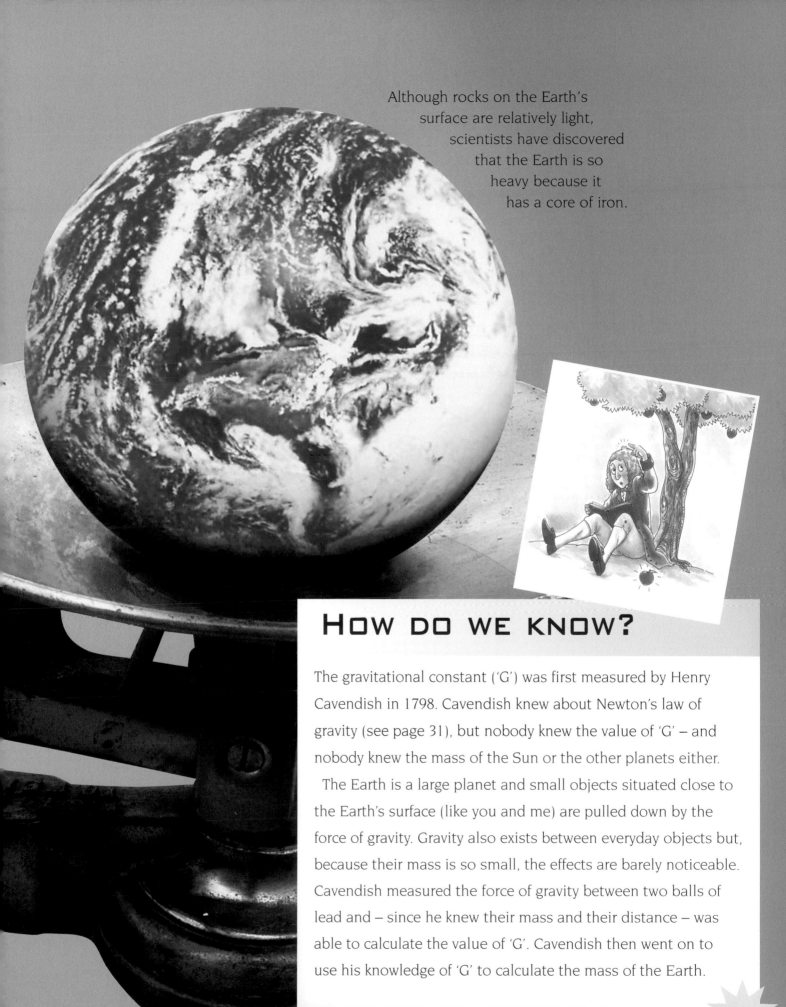

Although rocks on the Earth's surface are relatively light, scientists have discovered that the Earth is so heavy because it has a core of iron.

HOW DO WE KNOW?

The gravitational constant ('G') was first measured by Henry Cavendish in 1798. Cavendish knew about Newton's law of gravity (see page 31), but nobody knew the value of 'G' – and nobody knew the mass of the Sun or the other planets either.

The Earth is a large planet and small objects situated close to the Earth's surface (like you and me) are pulled down by the force of gravity. Gravity also exists between everyday objects but, because their mass is so small, the effects are barely noticeable. Cavendish measured the force of gravity between two balls of lead and – since he knew their mass and their distance – was able to calculate the value of 'G'. Cavendish then went on to use his knowledge of 'G' to calculate the mass of the Earth.

How do we know?

For hundreds of years, scientists have been investigating the origin of geographical features found on Earth. It used to be difficult to test their theories because they only had the Earth to study! However, in the last 30 years, researchers have begun testing their theories on other planets and moons – orbiting satellites have taken photographic images of the planets and bounced radio waves off their surface to measure structural features, including Olympus Mons. We have discovered more about Mars because there is so little atmosphere obscuring its surface. Scientists are currently mapping the surface of the planet using a space probe called the Mars Global Surveyor. Mars has examples of almost all the geographical features that we see on Earth. However, although there almost certainly was water on Mars in the past, today it is only in the form of ice, frozen under the surface and at the poles.

In 1969, a physicist called Weisskopf asked himself whether there was a limit to a mountain's height. He realised that if a mountain got too tall, its weight would melt the rocks at its base. Weisskopf estimated that the tallest mountain would have a height of 44 km on Earth and 1,600 km on Mars. Yet, Mauna Kea on Earth is 10 km tall and Olympus Mons is 'only' 24 km tall!

So why haven't these mountains grown taller? The most likely explanation is that if the mountains are volcanoes they are already warm. If the rocks contain water, they will also melt at a much lower temperature.

THE TALLEST KNOWN VOLCANO IS ON MARS

Olympus Mons is the largest mountain in the Solar System. Rising 24 km above the surrounding plain on Mars, its base is more than 500 km in diameter (almost as big as France) and its rim is a cliff 6 km high. Yet how did astronomers come to discover this monstrosity? And how did they measure its mighty size?

Although the Earth is the most geographically active planet in the Solar System, other planets have shown evidence of volcanic activity. A range of volcanoes, known as Maxwell Montes, have been discovered on Venus, reaching over 11 km above the surface of the planet. Io, a moon of Jupiter, also has active volcanoes that throw sulphur over 400 km into space. Olympus Mons would have formed in the same way as some of the more classic volcanoes found on Earth. Years ago, sticky lava from the rocks below Mars' surface erupted and solidified to form this huge volcano.

Yet, why does the Earth produce significantly more geological activity than the other planets? The reason lies in a combination of heat and water. When rocks are heated they become less dense and gradually rise. Water in rocks also makes them easier to melt and therefore flow. Planets like Venus, Mercury and Mars have no liquid water. Mercury and Mars are smaller than the Earth and they have lost most of their heat into space. Although Venus has lots of stored heat, conditions on the planet keep this heat under the surface. Moons like Io are unusual because they are being heated by the tidal forces of the large planets that they orbit.

Olympus Mons viewed from space (top left) alongside three smaller volcanoes known as the Tharsis triple.

IF YOU COULD DRIVE TO THE SUN IT WOULD TAKE 200 YEARS

Everybody knows that the Sun is a really long way away. The Sun is a massive star, but when we see it shining brightly in the sky it looks relatively small. But how far away is the Sun and how on earth do we actually measure this vast distance?

The Universe is so big that we are unable to measure it accurately in kilometres. We don't know exactly how big the Universe is, but from what we can see, even if you could travel at the speed of light, it would take at least 15 billion years to cross it!

HOW DO WE KNOW?

Over 300 years ago, a scientist called Cassini used a simple trick to measure the distance from the Earth to the Sun. If you hold your thumb at arm's-length and close one eye at a time, you'll see that your thumb moves against the background of distant objects. This effect is called 'parallax'. Cassini found that if you measure the distance your thumb moves and you know how far apart your eyes are, you can calculate the length of your arm.

In the 18th century, astronomers already knew the angles and the relative scale of the Solar System, so Cassini began by measuring the position of Mars from two different places on Earth. Having calculated the distance of the Earth from Mars, Cassini used a mathematical principle called 'trigonometry' to work out that the Earth was 140 million km from the Sun – a figure that is very close to modern scientific calculations. Today, astronomers use a similar method to calculate the Earth-Sun distance but use Venus instead of Mars. They shine radio waves at planet Venus and time how long it takes them to bounce back to determine the distance to this planet (we can't bounce radio waves off the Sun directly because it doesn't have a solid surface).

We now understand that the
Earth orbits the Sun once a year and
simultaneously rotates once a day. The other planets
of our Solar System also orbit the Sun at different distances.

• The Sun is about 150 million km from the Earth.
• Riding on a bicycle, it would take you about 1,000 years to get to the
Sun, at 5 metres per second (m/s).
• A family car travelling at 25 m/s would take 200 years and a racing car
travelling at 50 m/s would take 100 years.
• A supersonic jet travelling at 500 m/s would take over 10 years to arrive.
• Even light takes about 8 minutes to get from the Sun to the Earth –
and it's travelling at 300 million metres per second!

For many years, scientists have been planning international space
missions to Mars. However, calculations show that the spacecraft
would take months to arrive. If we ever visited the moons of
Jupiter it would take over a year to get there. Travelling
to Saturn would take 6 years, Neptune would
take 30 years and Pluto would take
up to 60 years!

Planet	Average distance to the Sun
Mercury	58 million km
Venus	108 million km
Earth	150 million km
Mars	228 million km
Jupiter	778 million km
Saturn	1,427 million km
Uranus	2,871 million km
Neptune	4,497 million km
Pluto	5,913 million km

MAN-MADE OBJECTS ARE NOW EXPLORING BEYOND THE SOLAR SYSTEM

Humans have always had an insatiable desire to explore. In the 20th century, developments in science and technology meant that space exploration at last became a reality. The journey to discover the hidden depths of the night sky began as space probes explored the planets and men and women ventured into the depths of space itself.

THE SCIENCE OF...

The modern space age began in 1957 when the Soviet Union launched the first artificial satellite, Sputnik I, into Earth's orbit sending radio signals back to Earth for the first time. Within two years, unmanned spacecraft were sent to the Moon and by the end of the 1960s, astronauts had walked on the surface of the Moon and spacecraft had descended to the surface of Venus and Mars.

Today, many probes are still orbiting the planets and our Sun. The Pioneer 10 & 11 and Voyager 1 & 2 spacecraft were launched in the 1970s to investigate the 'gas giants' (see page 16), and in the late 1990s they travelled beyond the orbit of Pluto. The Pioneer craft have now travelled over 50 times further than the distance from the Earth to the Sun. However, the last recorded contact with either craft was in January 2003. The Voyager spacecraft are nearly twice as far away, but they continue to send back information (via radio telescopes) about the boundary between our Solar System and interstellar space.

The 1980s saw the development of the space shuttle, capable of ferrying people and equipment to and from space. Although space shuttles may be discontinued, plans for a series of robotic space shuttles are set to take space exploration to another level.

WOWZSAT!

OVER A MILLION PIECES OF 'SPACE JUNK' MAY BE ORBITING THE EARTH — FROM SATELLITE FRAGMENTS TO LOOSENED PAINT CHIPS. ABOUT 70,000 OBJECTS THE SIZE OF A POSTAGE STAMP HAVE BEEN DETECTED IN AN AREA 850-1,000 KM ABOVE THE EARTH.

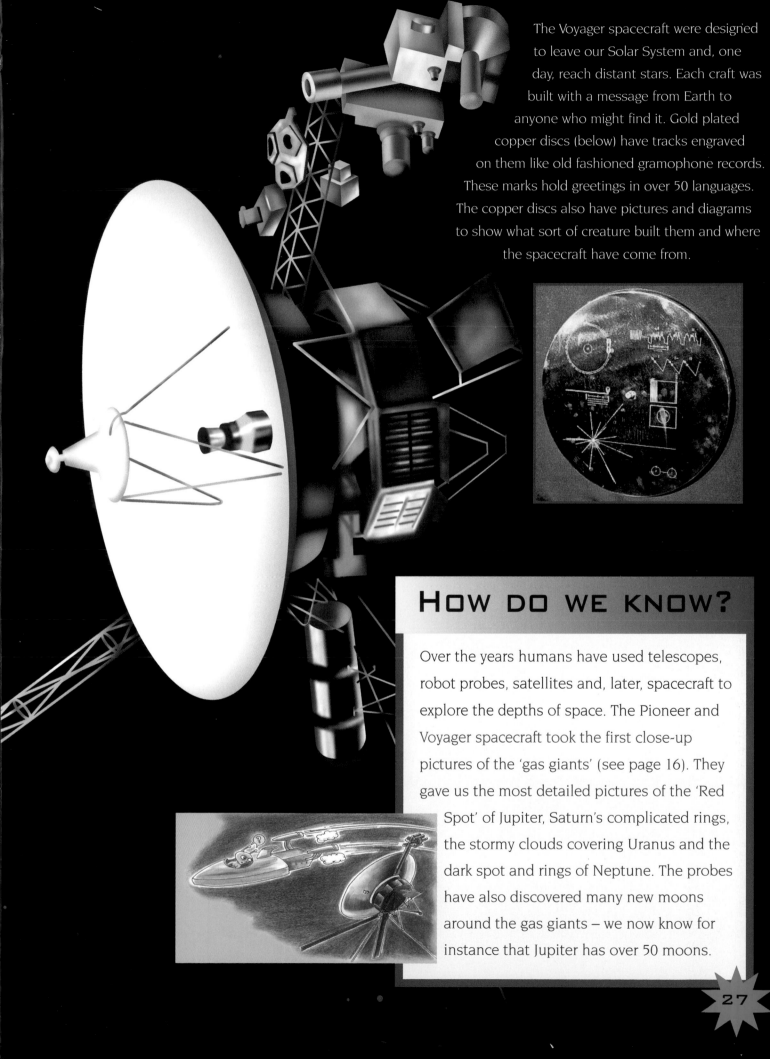

The Voyager spacecraft were designed to leave our Solar System and, one day, reach distant stars. Each craft was built with a message from Earth to anyone who might find it. Gold plated copper discs (below) have tracks engraved on them like old fashioned gramophone records. These marks hold greetings in over 50 languages. The copper discs also have pictures and diagrams to show what sort of creature built them and where the spacecraft have come from.

HOW DO WE KNOW?

Over the years humans have used telescopes, robot probes, satellites and, later, spacecraft to explore the depths of space. The Pioneer and Voyager spacecraft took the first close-up pictures of the 'gas giants' (see page 16). They gave us the most detailed pictures of the 'Red Spot' of Jupiter, Saturn's complicated rings, the stormy clouds covering Uranus and the dark spot and rings of Neptune. The probes have also discovered many new moons around the gas giants – we now know for instance that Jupiter has over 50 moons.

IN 2004 SCIENTISTS DISCOVERED A 10TH PLANET ORBITING THE SUN

In March 2004, scientists in America announced the discovery of a new planet orbiting the Sun. They christened the planet Sedna, after the Inuit goddess of the sea. This groundbreaking discovery highlighted the fact that our knowledge of the Universe is still limited. But is Sedna the 10th planet of our Solar System or is it (as some scientists believe) just another object orbiting our Sun?

THE SCIENCE OF...

In the last decade, scientists have discovered about 800 objects located beyond the orbit of Neptune. Most of these are about 100 km in diameter, but a few, like Sedna, are much bigger.

Scientists chose an Inuit (Arctic aboriginal) name because the planet is in a region of space surrounding our Sun, called the Oort cloud, which is incredibly cold. Measurements suggest that the rocks in the Oort cloud are colder than -250 °C. However, Sedna's official name is 2003 VB12 – a serial number used by astronomers to denote the year, month and approximate date that Sedna was first observed.

But is Sedna really a planet? Sedna is certainly large enough – at 1,700 km in diameter it is the biggest object found in our Solar System since Pluto. Measurements indicate that Sedna is over 12 billion km from the Sun – that's 80 times further than the Earth and two times further than Pluto. The planet debate still continues. Until it is resolved Sedna will be classified as one of a number of large objects that orbit the Sun in the Oort cloud.

HOW DO WE KNOW?

Uranus was discovered when William Herschel saw a disc (rather than a pinpoint) of light through his telescope. Subsequent studies of Uranus' motion proved that it was indeed the seventh planet. Pluto and Neptune were discovered when astronomers observed the unexpected movement of the planets closest to them. When successive photographs of the night sky showed an object wandering across the sky scientists attributed it to a planet orbiting the Sun. Sedna was discovered by chance when astronomers were studying objects on the edge of the Solar System. Sedna appeared as a moving dot on photographs taken over many months.

Mercury, Venus, Mars, Jupiter and Saturn can all be seen with the naked eye and have been known about for thousands of years. Uranus was first discovered in 1781. Neptune was officially recognised as a planet in 1846. Pluto was discovered in 1930 – exactly 149 years after the discovery of Uranus.

29

Glossary

Astronomer – A scientist who studies the Universe.

Atmosphere – The gas that surrounds a planet.

Atom – The smallest piece of a pure chemical element, e.g. hydrogen, oxygen or iron.

Black hole – A massive star that has collapsed and has so much mass that its force of gravity prevents everything escaping from it.

Centrifugal force – The force that appears to throw you outwards from an object that is spinning.

Cosmologist – A scientist who studies the evolution of the Universe.

Doppler Shift – The change in pitch of sound, or in the colour of light, when given out by a moving object.

Fusion – The process by which lighter atoms are combined to make heavier ones.

Gravity – The force that pulls all materials together across space.

Kilogramme (kg) – The scientific unit of mass.

Light-year – The distance travelled by light, through space, in one year: approximately ten million, million kilometres.

Nanometre (nm) – A nanometre is one millionth of a millimetre.

Newton (N) – The scientific unit of force.

Orbit – The path of an object as it travels around another object.

Planet – A large ball of gas or rock that orbits a star.

Radar – A technique used for measuring the distance (and/or speed) of an object by measuring the echo of a radio wave.

Radio wave – A low-energy form of light that we cannot see with our eyes.

Southern Hemisphere – The half of the Earth to the south of the equator. The term is also used to describe the southern half of the Sun and other planets and moons.

Space probe – A spacecraft that is designed to measure properties of the Universe.

Star – A large ball of gas (mainly hydrogen and helium).

Supernova – The massive explosion that occurs when stars bigger than our Sun have burnt most of their hydrogen.

Telescope – A device for making far-away objects look larger and brighter.

Universe – Absolutely everything that exists, including ourselves.

Weight – The force with which something is attracted to the Earth. Weight is measured in newtons, but we usually convert this to kilogrammes.

X-ray – A high-energy form of light that we cannot see with our eyes. X-rays can travel through many solid materials with ease.

Biography

Giovanni Cassini (1625-1712) An Italian astronomer who measured the direction of Mars from Paris and French Guiana (in South America). Cassini consequently calculated the distance from the Earth to the Sun.

Henry Cavendish (1731-1810) A British physicist who worked out the mass of the Earth by measuring the gravitational constant ('G').

Christian Doppler (1803-1853) An Austrian physicist who discovered that a change of frequency in sound waves was due to the relative motion of the source or observer.

William Herschel (1738-1822) A British astronomer who discovered Uranus in 1781.

Sir Isaac Newton (1642-1727) A British scientist and mathematician who proposed three laws of forces and motion. Newton also proposed a universal law of gravity – Force of gravity = G x (Mass1/distance) x (Mass2/distance).

Victor Weisskopf (1908-2002) An Austrian physicist who emphasised the importance of using basic knowledge in physics as a means to make reasonable estimates, such as calculating the maximum height of a mountain.

KEY DATES

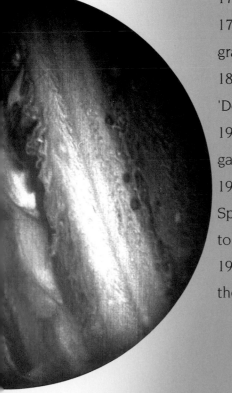

1054 – A supernova is observed.

1608 – The telescope is invented.

1781 – Herschel discovers Uranus.

1798 – Cavendish measures the gravitational constant.

1842 – Doppler proposes the 'Doppler Shift'.

1923 – The Hubble telescope shows galaxies outside the Milky Way.

1957 – The artificial satellite, Sputnik I, becomes the first object to orbit the Earth.

1961 – Yuri Gagarin becomes the first man to orbit the Earth.

1969 – Neil Armstrong and Edwin Aldrin become the first men to walk on the Moon.

1976 – The US Viking probes land on Mars.

1981 – The space shuttle is invented.

2004 – The discovery of a 10th planet, Sedna, is announced.

Index